ENTP

Understanding & Relating with

the Inventor

MBTI Personality Types Series

By: Clayton Geoffreys

Table of Contents

Foreword 1

An Introduction to MBTI 3

The Four Dimensions of the MBTI 9

   1.   Extraversion (E) vs. Introversion (I)..............10

   2.   Sensing (S) vs. Intuition (N) 13

   3.   Thinking (T) vs. Feeling (F) 15

   4.   Judging (J) vs. Perceiving (P) 18

Why is the Myers-Briggs Type Indicator Significant?
....23

   Career 24

   Relationships 28

   Self-Esteem 30

   Happiness 33

   Health and Longevity 36

Uncovering the "Inventor": Who is an ENTP?..........38

Why are ENTPs Indispensable Leaders? 42

The 9 Greatest Strengths of an ENTP 47

    1.   Visionary..47

    2.   Charismatic 49

    3.   Fearless 51

    4.   Great Communicator......................................53

    5.   Intelligent..54

    6.   Sense of Humor 55

    7.   Not Afraid To Fail 57

    8.   Not Easily Rattled...58

    9.   Excellent at Managing Stress........................59

The 6 Greatest Areas of Improvement for an ENTP..62

    1.   Impulsive 62

    2.   Disorganized 64

3.   No Follow Through 65

4.   Ignore Feelings 66

5.   Innovates for the Sake of Innovating 68

6.   Takes Dangerous Risks 69

What Makes an ENTP Happy? 72

What are Some Common Careers for an ENTP? 75

Politician 76

Scientist 76

Actor/Stand-Up Comedian 77

Comedy Writer 78

Professor 79

Inventor 80

Lawyer 80

Inspirational Speaker 81

Talk Show Host 82

Entrepreneur 83

Sales 84

Executive 84

Stock Broker/Venture Capitalist 85

Journalist 85

Consultant...86

Common Workplace Behaviors of an ENTP 88

ENTPs and Personal Relationships 91

Parenting Style & Values 91

Friends..94

Romantic Partners 95

8 Actionable Steps for Overcoming Your Weaknesses as an ENTP 100

1.   Find the Right Mate 100

2.   Mind the Details.........................101

3.   Pick Your Battles 102

4.   Respect the Contribution of Others 103

5.   Use Your Talents Wisely 104

6.   Consider the Feelings of Others 105

7.   Make Compromises 106

8.   Follow Rules 107

The 12 Most Influential ENTPs We Can Learn From 109

1.   Barack Obama 110

2.   Thomas Edison 111

3.   Walt Disney 111

4.   Benjamin Franklin 112

5.   Leonardo da Vinci 112

6.   Jon Stewart 113

7.   Bill Maher 114

8. Richard Feynman..115

9. Chairman Mao 115

10. Julia Child...116

11. Socrates...117

12. Theodore Roosevelt 118

Conclusion...119

Final Word/About the Author 121

Bibliography..124

Foreword

Have you ever been curious about why you behave certain ways? Well I know I have always pondered this question. When I first learned about psychology in high school, I immediately was hooked. Learning about the inner workings of the human mind fascinated me. Human beings are some of the most impressive species to ever walk on this earth. Over the years, one thing I've learned from my life experiences is that having a high degree of self-awareness is critical to get to where you want to go in life and to achieve what you want to accomplish. A person who is not self-aware is a person who lives life blindly, accepting what some label as fate. I began intensely studying psychology to better understand myself, and through my journey, I discovered the Myers Brigg Type Indicator (MBTI), a popular personality test that distinguishes between sixteen types of individuals. I hope to cover some of the most prevalent personality types of the MBTI test and share my findings with you through a series of books. Rather than just reading this for the sake of reading it though, I want you to reflect on the information that will be shared with you. Hopefully from reading *ENTP: Understanding & Relating with the Inventor*, I can pass along some of the abundance of information I have learned about ENTPs in general, how they view the world, as well as their greatest strengths and weaknesses. Thank you for purchasing my book. Hope you enjoy and if you do, please do not forget to leave a review!

Also, check out my website at claytongeoffreys.com to join my exclusive list where I let you know about my latest books. To thank you for your purchase, you can go to my site to download a free copy of *33 Life Lessons: Success Principles, Career Advice & Habits of Successful People*.

Cheers,

Clayton Geoffreys

An Introduction to MBTI

While we have many things in common with one another, no two people are alike.

Our appearances differ. We have different languages, dialects, and accents, and we have different beliefs about the world.

However, the most significant ways in which we differ are not down to looks, or membership in a church, or how we say hello. The most notable difference between two people is personality.

Two people can share the same language, culture, hair color, or religion, and yet be entirely different in how they interact with others and the world around them. In fact, two people can share the same *DNA* and still have wildly varying personalities—just ask any pair of identical twins!

Differences are a good thing. The variety of different traits we have makes the human race, culture, and society on a global level so vibrant.

In fact, if we were not so diverse, society as we know it could not exist. We need our diversity to allow us to fulfill the innumerable roles that *must* be filled to achieve the greatness the human race is capable of. Different roles require different skills, styles of thinking, and personalities.

How much could a society filled with only lawyers accomplish? Where would they live? What would they eat? Likewise, a society of only farmers would find it difficult to get around without engineers to design and build vehicles. Without writers and historians, how would we build on the past? Without teachers, how would our next generation find *their* place in society?

The point of this is that when we discuss two different poles in one of the personality dimensions, there is not an "inferior" or "superior" preference. It is vital to understand how each term is used in the context of this book to avoid that misconception. For example, the "judging" preference is not about being "judgmental." The terms used here often have a slightly different connotation than you might be used to in daily conversation.

While differences are not a matter of superiority or inferiority, they *are* sometimes a source of conflict. Differences in the ways we think and perceive the world can lead to misunderstandings. We may be too quick to decide that a person is wrong simply because they see the world in a different way. We have a set idea in our heads about what kinds of people are best. It is probably not surprising that we often think that people more like ourselves are the better people. We assign a value to different personality traits based on our personal comfort with them, and then we rank people based on how closely they conform to our ideas about "good" traits and "bad" traits.

These types of qualitative judgments lead to disagreements, persecution, lack of cooperation, and the inability to achieve goals together.

Of course, some of our great thinkers have contemplated these differences and how they affect our interactions with one another. Carl Jung was one such thinker, and his studies in the field of personality would go on to inspire and influence many others. Which is a great thing, because more often than not, simply *understanding* our differences can dissolve a conflict.

Isabel Myers and Elizabeth Briggs were two people inspired by Jung's work. In 1980, Isabel and her mother, Elizabeth, published a book entitled, *Gifts Differing,* which introduced the now famous Myers-Briggs Type Indicator (MTBI) — one of the most accurate and widely-used personality tests in the world.

They demonstrated that people are not only different but that each one of us has a different purpose in the world. Moreover, they stated that our goal should not be to divide, but to celebrate what makes us special and fulfill our unique purpose. Furthermore, the MTBI provides a guide for communication and helps us to understand why people do and say things in the way they do. Ultimately, this mutual understanding can decrease the possibility of conflict. The work of Myers and Briggs proved that personality could be categorized according to archetypes—specifically, 16 different types. One might be inclined to assume that a concept as complicated as personality could not be defined in such a quantifiable way. However, among the 2.5 million people who take the MBTI test every year, a vast majority of them find the assessment to be almost eerily accurate. The MBTI gives us a framework to understand our differences, and thus, appreciate it. By understanding each other, we can decrease our anxiety towards people who think differently than us, and ultimately, treat each other better. Likewise, by celebrating our types, we can achieve greater success and live happier lives instead of trying to be what we think we should be, or what other people believe we should be.

The MTBI empowers us to be the best selves we can be. We no longer have to go against the current of expectations and can move towards our true direction. Thus, we can focus on fostering our inherent strengths, and thus, become happier and more active people.

The Four Dimensions of the MBTI

Each of the 16 types is composed of distinct characteristics. These features represent an individual's preferences within four categories, sometimes referred to as "dimensions." Each dimension has a spectrum, and an individual's preferences represent which end of that spectrum their behaviors and thoughts most closely match.

For example, when making a decision, does an individual prefer to gather what they think are relevant details and then be decisive, quickly moving on to the next challenge? Or do they prefer to take their time collecting information until they understand the "big picture?" If it is the former, they are a "judging" type, while the latter prefers "perceiving."

The other three dimensions have the following preferences: thinking/feeling, extraversion/introversion, and sensing/intuition. Because each of these dimensions refers to a different area of thought or behavior, any individual can have any combination of the above traits, which means that there are 16 distinct personality types.

The personality types are referred to as a set of four letters, with each letter representing one of the preferences above. Introversion is designated with an "I," extraversion with an "E," and so forth. Except for intuition (N), the chosen letters are the first letter of the word describing preference.

Although each distinction might seem simple enough on its own, the real magic happens when the dimensions interact with each other when you combine them for each type.

1. Extraversion (E) vs. Introversion (I)

This dimension describes the relationship that the individual has with their internal and external worlds, how these worlds affect their energy levels, and where they focus their energy. In the simplest terms, extroverts prefer to focus outwardly while introverts focus inwardly.

The terms extrovert and introvert are already a part of our common vocabulary, and in the context of MBTI, they have a very similar meaning. However, the essence of these two words is slightly more complex within the framework of the MBTI. In the MBTI, extraversion vs. introversion is not just about social demeanor, but also about how a person understands and processes the world. As explained by Isabel Briggs, extroverted types "cannot understand life until they have lived it," and introverted types "cannot live life until they understand it."

You can also define extraversion vs. introversion as the reservoir where a person gets their power and energy. Extraverted people look outside themselves to re-fuel by feeding on the life and energy of others. Introverted people, on the other hand, look within.

They need time to themselves in quiet contemplation to re-fuel their mental energy.

Extroverts process information through conversation and gathering the opinions of others. Introverts, on the other hand, would rather mull over something on their own to come up with a conclusion.

One misconception people might have about these terms is the idea that being an introvert means being shy, withdrawn, or socially anxious, while being an extrovert means being outgoing and confident, as well as unable to tolerate alone time or quiet activities. However, the truth is that both introversion and extraversion are healthy expressions of this personality dimension.

However, introverts can enjoy socializing, and extroverts can enjoy solitude. The difference between them is not necessarily their like or dislike of these types of activities, but whether these activities drain their energy or recharge them.

An introvert may love going to a birthday party, but after several hours, feels the need to spend some time at home reading to recharge. Likewise, an extrovert might enjoy a long solitary hike in the mountains but eagerly look forward to being energized by meeting up with friends for a bustling happy hour at the pub afterward.

2. Sensing (S) vs. Intuition (N)

You have probably heard the term intuition. In everyday life, we use the term intuition to describe the ability to understand something without conscious thought or hard evidence. "Sense," in everyday language, means to use one of our senses: sight, hearing, touch, smell, or taste, to directly perceive the world.

The meanings of these terms in the context of the MBTI are quite closely related to their usual meanings. Here is an example.

Imagine a couple shopping for houses. One of them walks into a house and instantly knows it is the "right" one, while the other is busy looking at floor plans and examining the basement walls for signs of dampness. The intuitive type is certain it must be right because he can imagine playing baseball in the yard with his future son. The sensing type, meanwhile, is taking a closer look at the kitchen cabinets to see if they will need to be replaced because she thinks they should take the cost of remodeling into consideration when comparing homes.

Her eyes widen with alarm when he tells her it is perfect when he has yet to see the last inspection report. He is frustrated that they have already lost the chance to bid on several houses within their budget because she will not commit to bidding until she knows just one more detail. But then she has another question that must be answered, too. And another.

One of them is an intuitive type, and the other one is a sensing type. The intuitive type will walk into a home and just get a sense of whether or not it feels right. They might say things like, "I feel at home here," or "this place has a good vibe."

The sensing person cannot make decisions that way. They will need to look at the appraisal and inspection reports before they can formulate an opinion. For them, life is measured and tangible. They cannot understand why a person would "follow their gut" or come to any conclusions without evidence. They like to understand the world in a concrete way — relying on their senses. Intuitive types think more abstractly and are comfortable with vague ideas and imagination.

Each type has its advantages and disadvantages. Intuitive types are often able to benefit from new opportunities that sensing types miss because they are willing to move quickly. On the other hand, intuitive types may find themselves in hot water because they have become so entranced by potential opportunities that they have disconnected a bit from reality.

3. Thinking (T) vs. Feeling (F)

Once again, we want to stress the subtle distinctions between the meanings of a term in the context of the personality text versus how it is used in everyday life. "Thinking" types are not necessarily more intelligent, nor are "feeling" types more emotional. In the MBTI this dimension *solely* describes someone's preferences in decision making.

Someone who is quite emotional when having a bad day may nevertheless prefer the "thinking" pole of this dimension to the "feeling" pole when making decisions. Likewise, someone who prefers cerebral entertainment to that which is more sentimental might still be a "feeling" type on this scale because of how they make decisions.

Feeling types make their decisions based on the concerns and perceived concerns of all those involved.

This may indeed include emotions, but it is just as likely to be the desire to find a good compromise. Feeling types want everyone to be satisfied—to them, that is how one judges whether the right decision has been made. Rather than emotional, you might say that they focus on the *personal.* Not just for themselves, but for others.

They believe that by exploring and understanding the interests and motivations of everyone involved in a situation, the best decision can be reached. They live by a set of values, and they seek harmony whenever possible. They prefer tact to blunt communication.

Feeling types may run into difficulties when they find that the facts do not match up to the motivations or intentions of people involved in a situation, or this may go over their heads entirely. Others might see them as being too idealistic.

Thinking types are just the opposite, of course. It is the impersonal aspects of a situation that they weigh more heavily when making a decision. They look for quantifiable facts and potential outcomes. They tend to use objective, overarching principles to form the basis for their decision.

Thinking types like to arrange lists of pros and cons. They may care, even quite deeply, about the concerns or interests of the people involved in a decision, but they do not feel like basing action on personal concerns is either fair or practical. Whenever possible, they look for a resolution that is consistent with their logical view of the world and trust that such resolutions are the fairest.

Thinking types can err by completely discounting the personal to the point that they make a decision that *no one* involved is satisfied with. Consider the parable of the two women who both claimed a baby as their own and the king who suggested they cut the child in half. That is an extreme example of a "thinking" type misstep. Others may perceive them as cold or heartless.

4. Judging (J) vs. Perceiving (P)

The final dimension is the way we process information. Everyone uses both perception and judgment. We first perceive our surroundings and take in information. Then, we assign judgment, giving value to what we see in those surroundings. For example, we might hear a car alarm (perception) and then assign a value to that noise. We might feel annoyed, frightened, or worried. Then, we decide that it is a negative sound (judgment).

Although everyone does both, some types lean more on one process or the other and spend more time either perceiving or judging. In the car alarm example, the perceiver might take a moment to scrunch up their nose in annoyance, close the window, or put on headphones.

They may not feel any particular way about the noise aside from noting that it is loud at this point, and move on with their tasks as planned. If they *are* interested in it, they will not make any decisions about its cause until they have a chance to look out the window and see which car is making the sound.

Then they may try to deduce a cause based on what they see. If they see someone hanging out by the car, they may wonder whether it is a car thief or the owner, who has set off the alarm by mistake. They will look at what the person is wearing, how they are behaving, and so on before they decide what they think about the situation.

Or they may think nothing at all, and just file the event away as an annoying noise. Either way, they feel no great compulsion to come to a conclusion about it.

Judgment types are far faster at coming to conclusions. Depending on their past experiences, they might think, "There is too much crime in this neighborhood," or,

"Mr. Johnson down the street needs to change the settings on his alarm."

They might also come to conclusions about what is going on like, "It is probably a break-in, and I should call the police," or, "It is probably just a cat." While the judging person is going through all of those thoughts, the perceiver is still simply having a look (or has already moved on).

In essence, the judging person feels compelled to assign value and meaning to the world around them. They depend heavily on their ability to come to quick, decisive conclusions. Others perceive them as being organized, orderly, and in control for this reason. They are uncomfortable with ambiguity and have a hard time letting go of things they do not understand or interacting with people who do not have strong opinions about things.

They want the external world to be under control, and they come across as very task oriented as a result.

Judging types love lists, and they like to finish their to-do list before engaging in any sort of recreation. They avoid procrastinating whenever they can.

However, they can become so focused on completing goals efficiently that they fail to assimilate new information, which can affect their performance.

Perceiving types, on the other hand, are all open eyes and ears. They are in no rush to bend the world to their ideals; in fact, they prefer to adapt to their environment rather than try to change it or make it more orderly. They are often seen as casual, fun loving, and open-minded, and indeed, they love unusual experiences and learning new things.

Work and play are not mutually exclusive to perceiving types because they are not as likely to label these things. They work in bursts that are often unplanned. Procrastination can be a flaw of theirs as a result. Another problem they face is remaining so open-minded or receptive to new information that they fail to be decisive enough to be effective at all.

On the other hand, the perceiver can experience the world without needing to arrive at a conclusion.

Why is the Myers-Briggs Type Indicator Significant?

Understanding personality can change our perception of the world. People are not inherently smart or dumb, mean or nice, successful or failures, or happy or unhappy. We do not need to assign moral values to different personality traits. *Differing Gifts* shows us that we all have strengths and weaknesses, and we all have the potential to fail or be successful. The key to success is not found in who we are, but in what we choose to do.

If you know your personality type, strengths, and weaknesses, you are better equipped to make sound choices about your place in the world. Thus, you will most likely be capable of choosing a career you will succeed in, a partner you will be compatible with, and a group of friends whose company you will enjoy— leading to an increase in overall life satisfaction.

You might also be more capable of forgiving yourself when you fail and be more forgiving of others as well. Not everyone is meant to be good at everything, and in the context of MBTI, it is okay not to be good at everything. We all have our place in the world, and each of us has our unique way to be successful and contribute to society.

Career

MBTI is perhaps the most frequently used test in career selection and workplace communication. Most people spend around a third of their life working, so whether we like it or not, career is a huge part of our lives. Some people view their work as a burden or a chore, considering it an unpleasant but unavoidable fact.

This is often because the job that they have does not suit them, their personality, or their goals. Those who have positions that are compatible with their personalities and goals look forward to going to work.

They value their career and find satisfaction in it for its sake.

If you find a career that maximizes your strengths and supports your preferences, you are much more likely to enjoy your work. Thus, you will feel less stressed and report greater life satisfaction. Not only that, but you will be more productive and a better employee. By now, you should be starting to understand why the MBTI is such a favorite tool for career placement.

Imagine if an introvert chose a job in sales and had to spend their day talking, or if an extrovert became a computer programmer and had to spend their day alone. In that third of their life, they would be going against the current of their natural selves. They work harder just to be less successful. If you are on the correct career path, you will experience less stress and greater success.

MBTI also helps us understand each other in the workplace. While you have the power to choose your friends and mate, co-workers, on the other hand, are thrown together for the purpose of getting a job done.

Naturally, there will be a variety of different personalities among co-workers. In fact, it is unavoidable in most cases because most successful businesses need to have a wide variety of different personality types on their staff to fulfill different roles.

These people with various types of personalities must learn to work together. The MBTI is an excellent tool for facilitating that. Understanding how we each relate to the external world, what we value in the decision-making process, how we perceive the world, and so forth, can help build bridges between people.

It can also give us a chance to gain new perspectives. A thinking type decision-maker might object to a feeling type decision-maker assigning a conference room too far away from one department.

However, if they are aware of different decision-making styles, they might ask the feeling type coworker and discover that the closer conference room has more accessible handicap parking needed by a different department for the same time slot.

The thinking type probably would not have taken the time to call up the various groups to find out if they had a preference, because to them, knowing impersonal information like the location of the rooms in relation to the departments' offices is sufficient.

On the other hand, the situation can also be entirely reversed. A feeling person might be upset that the thinker assigned them to the further conference room, not knowing if they checked the employee files for any accessibility issues for each department.

You may have noticed that in the situation above, the first and second decision maker came to the same solution despite a difference in preferences when it comes to decision-making.

This is not uncommon. Having opposite preferences does not mean that two people will always come to the opposite conclusion. It simply means that they will reach their conclusion—the same or different—by way of a different path.

In the first circumstance, the parking needs were presented as a personal concern, one that the decision-maker discovered by contacting the other people involved. The feeling type decision-maker is most focused on the concerns of the various parties.

In the second, the parking needs were presented as an impersonal fact. The thinking decision maker is not wondering about whether or not that department is or is not concerned about parking. They looked at the facts and chose the most efficient method of assigning adequate parking.

We used this example because we want to make it clear that although there is a sharp dichotomy between the two poles of any one of the personality dimensions, it does not mean that you will always *disagree* with someone of a different personality type.

Relationships

Some personality types will put more importance on love and relationships than others. Regardless, most of us desire a partner (or at least a series of partners!). We want intimacy, someone to share our hopes and dreams with, someone to care for us, and someone to care for.

Whether permanent or temporary, most of us will pair up with someone eventually. Romantic relationships can play a huge role in our happiness (or lack thereof).

A good marriage is widely considered one of the most important factors to determine happiness. Positive relationships have even been linked to better health, a stronger immune system, and an increased lifespan.

So, what makes a positive relationship?

To fully answer that question, we would have to write another book—a very long one! Nevertheless, in the context of this one, both personality compatibility and the ability to communicate and understand personality differences play a critical role in having a healthy relationship.

Understanding builds better communication and helps us to have greater respect for our partners. As we have touched on already, one of the most important steps toward understanding one another is being aware of personality differences and learning not to come to unnecessarily negative conclusions about them.

Understanding MBTI categories and personality types can help us find partners with whom we are more compatible. In addition to that, it can help us untangle disagreements and misunderstandings if our personality type and that of our partner do not necessarily align well. It is an excellent tool for both finding compatibility and overcoming incompatibility in our relationships.

Self-Esteem

It is hard to be happy or successful without healthy self-esteem. Everyone has some form of self-doubt, and most of us have some traits or characteristics that we do not like about ourselves or judge ourselves for having.

Viewing ourselves as being valuable to society and to the other people we encounter is important for several reasons. It is important for our emotional health and happiness, of course.

However, it is also important because when we see ourselves as valuable to society, we are more likely to do our best. It is quite difficult to give 110% at work or to help a friend if you believe you are worthless. Having a healthy self-esteem is not a selfish goal.

Some types are naturally more confident than others are, but anyone can suffer from low self-esteem if they do not understand their personal strengths. MBTI delivers strengths with each personality report.

All of the 16 types have a resume of desirable strengths. They just happen to differ from one another. By knowing which personality type describes them, people with low self-esteem will know exactly what they have to offer. They do not have to fake anything or pretend to be something they are not; they already have strengths just by being themselves. They also do not have to undergo the torture of comparing themselves to someone with an entirely different set of strengths and weaknesses.

Although it may seem counterintuitive at first, self-esteem can also come from understanding our weaknesses. Imagine a woman who was always pushed by her mother to be more social as a child. She forced her to go to parties, go on blind dates, and meet strangers. There was a never-ending stream of extracurricular activities.

At the end of each day, this little girl would practically collapse in her bedroom alone, feeling overwhelmed, drained, and fearful of disappointing others. She grew into a woman who believed she must be anti-social and could never be as likable or charming as someone more sociable.

However, once she took the MBTI, she learned that she was an introvert. There was never anything wrong with her—she just has a different orientation. She then no longer sees herself as "broken" and accepts introversion as a part of her personality without assigning judgment.

Now, she can happily attend a class reunion for an hour or two, chat confidently, and enjoy herself because she knows she has already got everything set up for a bubble bath and Netflix marathon when she gets home to recharge.

Happiness

People often consider the "pursuit of happiness" to be a romantic and existential notion, but social scientists have published hundreds of scholarly articles that essentially prove exactly what humans need to be happy. Relationships are a key factor, but "flow" is also significant.

Happiness is good for our bodies as well as our minds, and it makes us better members of society. The pursuit of happiness is not a hedonistic or selfish pursuit. It is merely the pursuit of being your best self and finding your place in the world.

Hungarian psychologist Mihaly Csikszentmihalyi is known for his description of the concept of "flow" as well as his studies in creativity and happiness. He believes that "life satisfaction" is most attainable when we can engage in activities that captivate us—that is, we lose track of time, our worries evaporate, and we are barely even aware of ourselves. It could be gardening, writing, or building a rocket. The key is just finding a task that brings them out of themselves.

Csikszentmihalyi described someone whom he felt had attained, perhaps, the highest level of happiness he had ever witnessed. The man was an old welder from

Chicago. He had only a fourth-grade education but was quite talented at his craft. His pride in welding resulted in his turning down the opportunity to advance to a position as supervisor because he would not have been able to weld actively. After a day of exhausting work, he would return home and spend his evening sitting in his rock garden. He had built the garden himself and set up lights and sprinklers that, together, created rainbows.

That man did something counterintuitive to happiness — he declined a promotion and more money. However, he made that choice because he understood his personality type. He knew he would be happier and more satisfied as a welder, and not a supervisor.

Perhaps that older gentleman is a sensing type, or an introvert, or both. He probably did not take the MBTI to figure out his sources of comfort and happiness, but it may have taken many years of trial and error.

By understanding our personality types and preferences, we can align our life choices with those options that best suit our personalities. We can place ourselves in situations where we will excel because of our personal strengths. We can work to better understand our partners and children, our coworkers and bosses, and we can help them better understand us.

Self-awareness is key to happiness, and the MBTI is a fantastic way to become more self-aware.

Health and Longevity

Behind all of our differences, we all want the same thing — to live a long and happy life. Stress from bad relationships, poor self-esteem, and inadequate careers can increase our risk of health problems and even early death. Although tangible healthy behaviors such as eating healthy and exercising have a noticeable impact on health and longevity, studies have also shown that more abstract factors, like happy relationships, healthy stress levels, and overall satisfaction with our lives can also affect our health and longevity.

This is probably due in part to the fact that unhappiness and chronic stress leads us to take on unhealthy behaviors like drinking, smoking, and overeating, which themselves result in health problems.

However, stress itself can contribute to disease, especially high blood pressure, heart attack, and stroke. The harder we fight against our natural personality type, the more wear and tear we put on our bodies and our minds. If you understand and respect your personality type, you could live longer and feel better. You will also be more motivated to take care of your body and mind, and you will have more energy to do so.

Understanding the MBTI is significant because it can lead us to find our "flow." It helps us to become more self-aware, which makes us better able to critically assess whether the "improvements" society presses on us (like a promotion, or living in a bigger house, or going out four nights a week, etc.) are going to make us happy.

Perhaps some of those things will, but maybe there are entirely different goals that are more likely to lead us to a happy, fulfilling life. The MBTI can help us become aware of them.

Uncovering the "Inventor": Who is an ENTP?

If you are an ENTP and feel like you have not met very many other people like yourself, well, you are probably not wrong. ENTP is one of the least typical of all the 16 personality types. ENTP comprises of only 3% of the general population, 4% of all men, and only 2% of women.

Each of the 16 personality types has their place in the world, and we need each one. Only a fraction of all people can fill the role that ENTPs have in society, so it is even more important that they learn to maximize their strengths and reach their potential.

ENTP stands for EXTRAVERTED, INTUITIVE, THINKING, and PERCEIVING.

Their extraversion makes them charismatic communicators and social butterflies. Their tendency toward intuition and perception over sensing and judging makes them fantastic abstract and out-of-the-box thinkers. They can see far beyond the tangible and are open to all sorts of new ideas. The thinking trait tempers this well, making them dreamers with a logical and objective thought process, which helps them turn their dreams into reality.

ENTPs are sometimes called "inventors" or "visionaries." Some of the world's most famous inventors and visionaries were ENTPs, including Thomas Edison, Benjamin Franklin, and Leonardo da Vinci. They are also the great thinkers of the world — philosophers like Socrates, Machiavelli, Voltaire, and David Hume. Imagine what the world would be like if those ENTPs never reached their potential.

While the rest of the world manages the mundane, routine tasks of day-to-day life, ENTPs are pondering the great questions and examining what it means to be human.

They are the larger-than-life, bold people that everyone wants to follow. They come up with new, innovative ideas that no one has tried before. They are not afraid of failure or risks and will keep trying until they succeed. All of these traits lead them to break barriers and instigate change.

Consider the famous ENTP, Walt Disney, who turned his dreams into reality at Disneyland Park. They are also the people who make us laugh. ENTPs have made us laugh on Monty Python, Saturday Night Live, The Daily Show, the Colbert Report, Late Night with Conan O'Brian, and many primetime sitcoms like Friends, How I Met Your Mother, Frasier, Will and Grace, and Parks and Recreation. They see the humor in even the darkest situations and are not afraid to take a risk with an edgy joke to get a big laugh.

Impressively successful, ENTPs not only have one of the highest average incomes among all the types, but they also have one of the lowest rates of heart disease and report fewer personal problems than other types. This is likely because ENTPs are typically excellent at finding their niche, and as a result, happiness and fulfillment.

They only make up a fraction of the population and have been responsible for a far greater percentage of innovation, creativity, and invention. It is crucial that we cultivate these intelligent minds because the ENTPs living today are the ones who will shape our future.

Why are ENTPs Indispensable Leaders?

ENTPs are not your ordinary leaders. They are not just suited to leading a few people here and there, or even a group of individuals. Their leadership has often had the power to change the world.

As leaders, their ability to think strategically while still being visionaries can lead their followers to accomplish incredible things. Creativity and innovation come naturally to them, and they are adept at identifying trends early and noting patterns before they are apparent to others. These abilities make it possible for ENTPs to lead sweeping, large-scale changes.

ENTP leaders are not interested in micromanaging their followers. Their focus is the "big picture," and they are irritated and uninterested when bogged down by small details. They are better in leadership roles than following positions for this reason, because while their broad perspectives make them excellent delegators, they find details aggravating. As a result, they tend to surround themselves with self-motivated followers that take the initiative to answer their own questions and work out minutiae on their own.

As leaders, ENTPs are unlikely to provide lots of direction or emotional support. Although extroverted, they make decisions based largely on their "thinking" preference. This leads them to rely on cold, hard facts more than the concerns of the people affected by their decisions. They may care deeply about those people, but the best, most fair and practical decisions are, according to ENTPs, made impersonally.

Therefore, they may not always be as diplomatic as some other types of leaders because ultimately they have their eye on the big picture. Their intuitiveness serves them well in that sense, but they can be blind to small details and reactions from their teams. Their mind is already in the future, and not with the seemingly trivial problems of the present. As one article states, "ENTPs make poor managers but exceptional leaders."

ENTPs do not require a title or status to step into a leadership role; they were born for it. Others recognize it and flock to them, and ENTPs are naturally comfortable with giving others direction—after all, they have long-term innovative goals that need achieving!

They are charismatic, confident, and have strong personalities, so people will naturally turn to them and follow them. They are great speakers and sparkle with charm.

Many believe President Barack Obama to be a fantastic example of an ENTP leader. He once described himself as an argumentative adolescent, prone to rebelling against rules that he considered "arbitrary" or "petty." He says that he was successful in his arguments more often than not. His powerful charisma and oral communication skills helped him become elected to the nation's highest office.

Other notable ENTP leaders include Newt Gingrich, Catherine the Great, Benjamin Franklin, Apple co-founder Steve Wozniak, Henry Kissinger, Dictator of Communist China Mao Zedong, and President Mahmoud Ahmadinejad of Iran.

It is also important to note that ENTPs are good traditional leaders of people and nations, but they can also be the leading edge of social change. Our history has been marked by critical ENTP inventors, philosophers, and artists that lead in less traditional but perhaps even more important, ways.

These ENTP leaders change how the world works and how people think. They have included such historically and culturally significant names as Socrates, Leonardo da Vinci, Thomas Edison, physicist Richard Feynman, Voltaire, and Niccolo Machiavelli.

Leaders such as these demonstrate why ENTPs are so important for society. They see things differently. They see the bigger picture and can think in new ways—ways that sometimes drastically change the world we live in.

The 9 Greatest Strengths of an ENTP

There is nothing narcissistic about knowing and understanding your strengths. Knowing your strengths will help you become confident and genuine. This will help you prepare to sell yourself in job interviews and life in general.

Knowing your strengths is also helpful when you find yourself in a bind. If you are in a difficult situation and you are trying to decide between several different solutions, knowing your strengths can help you choose the right one.

The solution is often one that plays to your strengths— you are more likely to be successful if you rely on your strengths than try an iffy solution where one of your weaknesses might turn out to be a critical flaw.

1. Visionary

ENTPs are simply not bound by the limitations of the world or society. Their lack of respect for limits or rules can cause personal problems, but can also lead to breakthroughs and innovation. Naysayers, old-fashioned thinkers, obstacles, unanticipated problems—none of these things can dissuade an ENTP from achieving their goal.

In addition to being visionary thinkers and innovators, they are also fabulously creative. ENTPs often make great writers and filmmakers. They are driven by imagination and can see the world for more than what is right in front of them.

Do not make the mistake of assuming an ENTP is just a daydreamer, however. They can be profoundly logical, and this combined with their unparalleled persistence means that they rarely give up on a goal. Sentimental reasons will not turn them aside, and practical problems are often mowed down in front of them like grass in front of a mower.

ENTP Walt Disney once famously said, "If you can dream it, you can do it," and he did not just say it to make a great sound bite. No, Disney is the quintessential example of an ENTP. Visionary, creative, persistent, unstoppable, and a logical, formidable businessman.

The world is full of possibilities for an ENTP. They do not just see the world as it is today; they see the world as it could be.

2. Charismatic

ENTPs are the type of people that others describe as having "a certain something" or a "sparkle." ENTPs naturally draw others into their circle—in fact, they do not have to draw them in, because other people compete for their attention. ENTPs have to do little if any actual work to have this effect on other people because the behaviors and ideas that come naturally to them do it for them. Their effortless charisma is one of their most distinct qualities.

This charisma does more than making them famous. It also projects an air of confidence that inspires trust and loyalty in others. Sometimes, it can even prompt others to behave more passively or submissively to let the ENTP have their way.

ENTPs have an aura around them that proclaims "I know what I am doing, follow me," and many people respond to it. When you see someone monopolizing a conversation, and it seems like everyone in the group is okay with it—or even encouraging it—you might be looking at an ENTP.

It is rare to see an ENTP that is uncomfortable in social situations for these reasons. Not only do they thrive on the company of others, but people also go out of their way to accommodate them. That is not to say that ENTPs are bullies. Their company is highly coveted by others, and they cherish the opportunity to exchange ideas or even have a heated debate with just about anyone.

Whether they are chatting with someone one or one or captivating an entire room full of people, ENTPs are in their element as long as they are the center of attention.

Public speaking is a natural thrill for ENTPs, as is performing. They can feel the energy of their audience and harness it. That is why you will find so many ENTPs on stage.

3. Fearless

Courage is one of the things that make ENTPs such formidable visionaries and inventors. They are not afraid to go where no one has gone before and taken risks. You will not necessarily find them jumping out of planes or climbing a mountain — although they probably would not say no if you offered — but they prefer other types of risks. They are not precisely daredevils — not because of fear, but because they are more interested in inherent risks.

That is because ENTPs are not adrenaline junkies. Their willingness to take risks is a combination of their fearlessness and desire to see the results, so unnecessary risks do not beguile them. ENTPs take the best kinds of risks, the ones supported by logic and planning. They do not care about taking risks just for the thrill or rush — they take the risks that need to be taken to meet their goals.

As philosophers, inventors, and theoretical scientists, they take intellectual risks more than physical ones. They are not afraid to think outside the box or defy traditional beliefs. If the world is not flat or the sun does not revolve around the earth, ENTPs will be the first ones to tell you; and they are not afraid of the repercussions of that new idea.

There is another area in which ENTPs' fearlessness serves them well: they are not scared of arguments or conflict. In fact, they enjoy a good debate and are often open about that enjoyment. And while they usually have strong opinions about things (and are often right), they also do not fear bein wrong.

Being challenged, criticized, or even chastised will not put an ENTP off of a conversation, or even put them in a bad mood. Their ability to look at issues impersonally when making decisions applies to themselves as well—they can look at the argument and the various positions in an impersonal way. They are great at taking constructive criticism, which makes them well-suited to challenging and breaking intellectual barriers.

4. Great Communicator

If you are looking for an ENTP, you might check the debate team. They are excellent oral communicators who thrive in good, spirited arguments. Give them a few minutes to talk, and they can convince you of almost anything. Put them behind a podium and they might even change the world.

They communicate well in formal settings, like giving speeches or participating in a debate, but they also excel at interpersonal communication. They are masters of conversation. If you are at a party, find the ENTPs. Happy to discuss any topic, they make for great company. It would not be unreasonable for them to talk for hours just enjoying the conversation and the company.

Although they love to talk, they will not waste words. They get straight to the point and are always clear and concise, which is another thing that makes them an excellent communicator. There is never any doubt about the message they want to convey.

5. Intelligent

ENTPs value knowledge and intellect. They are often considered great thinkers. Their combined love of logic with the ability to intuitively sense the big picture is a formidable combination. Their open-mindedness, desire to learn, and willingness to talk to others about anything and everything means that they have a very broad range of knowledge. Not only that, they *love* to share it.

Most of all, ENTPs love to *use* their knowledge. They like to apply what they have learned, and more often than not, they apply it innovatively and creatively.

Invention and discovery are intoxicating to ENTPs. They love to approach facts, ideas, and theories in new ways to come up with different interpretations and applications.

Inventing gives ENTPs the chance to put their considerable intellects to work *and* an excuse to show off and be the center of attention. Because they are not concerned about criticism, they will often return to the drawing board repeatedly until they succeed. They are not discouraged by a setback, or a dozen setbacks.

This persistence makes ENTPs so effective at invention that they are known as "the inventors" in the MBTI community. It is, after all, rare that a unique, one-of-a-kind invention would work perfectly the first time around, or that everyone would support a new and strange idea. These obstacles put off many other types of personalities, but they are barely even a blip on the ENTP's radar.

6. Sense of Humor

ENTPs see the world in new and creative ways. Humor is often based on an element of surprise. Using a word in a surprising context or in a way in which it is not usually meant or providing an ending to a story with a twist can make people laugh.

All of these elements of humor depend on being able to see things from a different perspective, and ENTPs are excellent in that regard. They are also able to see humor in situations that others might miss. They come to amusing conclusions and see clever connections in the everyday world.

Likewise, their communication and conversation skills help them convey their humor in the most eloquent and witty way. Their knowledge and intellect allow them to come up with smart jokes such as political humor. However, they love the attention of others and appreciate any kind of humor that gets them a big laugh.

If you have any doubt that ENTPs make good comedians, look at the impressive list of hilarious ENTPs in popular media: Jon Stewart, Stephen Colbert, Sacha Baron Cohen of Borat, John Cleese of Monty Python, Rowan Atkinson of Mr. Bean, Neil Patrick Harris, David Hyde Pierce of Frasier, Amy Poehler, Megan Mullally, Conan O'Brian, and Matthew Perry.

Take a moment to consider what primetime and late night television would be without ENTPs. We would also be without classic comedic groundbreakers like Monty Python (both John Cleese and Terry Gilliam are ENTPs).

7. Not Afraid To Fail

Famous ENTP Thomas Edison said it best with his famous quotes, "Genius is 1% inspiration and 99% perspiration," and "I have not failed. I have just found 10,000 ways that will not work." As is typical of an

ENTP, he does not sound at all perturbed by the fact that he had so many setbacks!

This particular attribute is one of the reasons why ENTPs make fantastic inventors. No successful invention has come without many failures. Think about all the planes that did not fly, all the light bulbs that did not light, and all the phones that did not ring before those groundbreaking inventions were successful.

The willingness of ENTPs to fail is exactly what makes them so successful in so many ways. That willingness to fail is paired with an unstoppable persistence. The bottom line is that if ENTPs were afraid to fail, our world would be a very different, and possibly much darker, place.

8. Not Easily Rattled

ENTPs love debate so much that they argue for fun. That is right — they enjoy arguing — a concept that sounds ridiculous to many other types, especially introverts. Although that might sound like an aggravating trait (and it can be in some contexts!), it speaks of one of their powerful strengths. ENTPs are not easily offended, upset, or rattled. Conflict and opposing viewpoints do not get them down. Instead, they thrive on opposition.

This is another reason why ENTPs are so successful. No one does anything worthwhile in the world without some criticism along the way. Anyone in the public eye these days is going to get a thorough bashing on social media no matter what they do. Trolls or anyone else out to get them down do not bother ENTPs. They are confident, and their self-esteem is not easily battered. This is critical for all ENTP politicians, actors, and comedians.

ENTP President Barack Obama would not be able to function if he was easily bothered by criticism. ENTP talk show hosts and political commentators like Jon Stewart and Bill Maher have to be comfortable enough with conflict to argue passionately with their opponents on national television, something that sounds like a nightmare to some other personality types!

9. Excellent at Managing Stress

Of all the types, ENTPs are rated among the best at managing stress. They generally report fewer personal problems and have a relatively low rate of heart disease.

ENTPs do well at coping with stress, but more importantly, they view stress in a more productive way than other types. They see conflict, failure, and adversity as a natural part of success.

Setbacks do not get them down. Instead, setbacks push them to work harder. Because of this general attitude toward stress, they can manage all sorts of challenges that would cripple other types.

The great Walt Disney once pointed out that even he—

successful as he was—had experienced a great deal of adversity. Rather than bemoan the obstacles he would have had to overcome or the challenges that troubled him, he saw them as a source of strength. When others were down and out, he would tell them that while it feels awful at the time, sometimes a "kick in the teeth" could be one of the best things that can happen to you.

For ENTPs, the sky is not the limit. There is no limit to what they can achieve if their strengths are appropriately cultivated. Society benefits when we understand the value and importance of the ENTP personality type.

The 6 Greatest Areas of Improvement for an ENTP

As they say, the bigger they are, the harder they fall. ENTPs can fly high and fall very hard. In short, they are not afraid to fail, and as such, they do fail, and often. While this is an integral part of their ability to succeed at innovation, it also puts them at risk.

Sometimes they fail big. ENTPs are big-picture thinkers, but they ignore the small pictures, and those "minor" details are sometimes crucial.

They love a good argument, even if the other person is not having as much fun as they are. Despite being highly successful human beings, ENTPs have some significant and potentially dangerous flaws that they need to be aware of so they can appropriately manage them.

1. Impulsive

The innovative, risk-taking qualities that can make ENTPs meteoric successes can also make them spectacular failures. It all depends on whether or not the impulse was a good one. ENTPs are not afraid to take risks, fail, and be wrong. Sometimes, this means they take risks that they should not. They could fail in dangerous ways, or they are wrong about something critically important.

When they fail, they may not be willing or able to clean up the mess. They lack organizational skills and ignore important details. When they make a mistake, they may bring their group of loyal followers down with them. They do this with little understanding of how they were hurt and leave them to clean up after them.

This can especially be a problem in the workplace where ENTPs may act on impulse in areas where they are not authorized to, or make decisions that should have been seconded by a superior. The problem is compounded by the fact that even if something goes wrong, ENTPs are not bothered much by failure, so they are often not particularly contrite.

2. Disorganized

Although brilliant in many ways, the ENTPs can be dunces when it comes to basic tasks. They are messy, disorganized, procrastinators, and bad at time management. The cause of all of these is a lack of respect for details. Whether the dishes are done — and perhaps even whether the bills are paid — or not is not critical to their master plan, and their master plan (or several master plans!) are always at the forefront of their minds.

They may not respect the deadlines and structures that others impose on them. They may appear to be procrastinating or using time poorly, but to them, it is simply that they have chosen to use their time in a different way.

An ENTP scientist, artist, or philosopher may spend hours, or even years, pondering on abstract concepts with little impact on their life. They may tinker with an idea that has little chance of success because it fits their vision. At the same time, they might ignore the real problems right in front of their face, like a home that needs cleaning or repairs.

Sometimes it seems as if ENTPs each need a partner, sidekick, or personal assistant who can take care of their daily needs while they ponder their dreams and ideas.

3. No Follow Through

ENTPs are "idea" people, and that is it. They have little to no interest in the practical application of their thoughts. By the application phase, the ENTP has already moved on to the next idea in their mind. This is partly because they always have so many ideas swimming around in their heads. However, there is another factor as well. Many ENTPs learn quickly when they are young that they are not detail oriented.

Their various ideas and dreams can be too much that they often find it difficult to focus on one thing. They are easily bored and will quickly move on to new ideas. For this reason, they are perhaps too reliant on other types for their success. ENTPs cannot make change without other, more practical types following behind them, managing details and getting things done.

When an ENTP has a team that they can delegate to, they can shine very brightly, however.

Notable ENTP, Walt Disney, recognized his reliance on others, saying, "You can design, create, and build the most wonderful place in the world. But it takes people to make the dream a reality."

4. Ignore Feelings

Although very sociable, ENTPs do not consider personal concerns in their decisions. They are "thinkers" as opposed to "feelers," so they do not value the importance personal issues in conflicts or decisions unlike many other personality types. This trait combined with their direct and dominant nature can lead them to say hurtful things. Because they are so rarely offended and do not find criticism or bluntness hurtful, they may not understand what they have done to upset the other party.

Additionally, their Type A qualities and strong personalities can cause them to run over less aggressive personality types, leaving introverts and feeling types in their wake. ENTPs love to argue and thrive on conflict. They might not be aware that others do not share their passion. Likewise, they may not understand that other people are not as calm under pressure and comfortable with criticism as they are.

They are not afraid of taking risks, including in conversations. Because of these reasons, ENTPs may unintentionally shut down conversations with other personality types. Thoughtful ENTPs are cognizant of these issues, but others may brush them off by calling others "too sensitive."

Charisma has its dark side, too. Their dominance in personal situations and golden tongue can slide into the realm of intimidation, control, and manipulation. They love humor and practical jokes. However, occasionally, those jokes are at the expense of others.

The ENTP often considers the feelings of others as insignificant details that might get in the way of their far more important goals and tasks. This view of the world can quickly make them seem rude and uncaring.

5. Innovates for the Sake of Innovating

ENTPs love to "re-invent the wheel." That is, they will innovate things that do not need to be simply because they are bored with the original. Innovation has an important place, but there is nothing wrong with the tried and true. Sometimes things are a classic for a reason—they work. Unconventional thinking is great, but there is no reason to dismiss the traditional without valid and significant grounds.

Sometimes, certain rules and policies are in place for a very good reason. Standards and laws hold our society intact, and most of them serve a useful purpose. However, ENTPs do not respect rules or boundaries in general.

They might think they know better, and ignore arguments that are contrary to what they believe in, assuming that people who like the old way of thinking are simply closed-minded or old-fashioned. ENTPs assume that the new way, or more specifically, their way, is the best way. As such, they will reject opinions contrary to their belief.

More problematically, sometimes they just refuse to obey rules or policies due to a sort of warped principle. They do not obey them because they do not want to—even if they see the value in the rule or policy for others. This can lead to unnecessary conflicts and problems with authority figures.

6. Takes Dangerous Risks

Risk-taking is one of the things that make the ENTP such a fantastic inventor and innovator. They are not afraid to fail – even fail big. Naturally, this risk-taking can have a dark side. ENTPs are not necessarily jumping out of planes and risking physical harm, but they can cause significant harm to themselves and others.

Sometimes the impossible is impossible. The ENTPs belief that boundaries do not apply can lead them to be foolishly risky. Imagine them as men who believe they can fly, strap on paper wings, and jump off a building. No amount of belief can actually make them not hit the pavement with great force.

ENTPs can make risky career moves and devastating financial decisions. Who knows how much money has been spent on ENTPs' dreams and far-fetched ideas that did not pan out? For every Thomas Edison, how many inventors died hungry and in obscurity while their families struggled?

ENTPs with a family can make a risky investment and devastate the family finances. ENTP executives can pool too much money into a pet project and lead the company to financial disaster, perhaps even emptying pensions.

A risk simply is not a risk if there is not a good chance of significant loss. ENTPs are unlikely to make it through life without at least one major failure, and they can only hope that their risk does not harm too many innocent bystanders in the process.

While ENTPs often have groundbreaking visions of what can be and can take risks others would not dream of and find success, their fearlessness can be a pitfall in this respect.

Every one of the 16 personality types comes with a list of flaws. Some of us may want to determine which flaws are "worse" than others, but the spirit and intention of the MBTI are to celebrate each type and honor their role in society. In the case of ENTPs, they must simply be aware of their flaws so they can manage them to keep them from becoming obstacles to success.

What Makes an ENTP Happy?

There are certain universal components to happiness across all types—things such as positive relationships and good career fit. However, ENTPs are an excellent example of how a personality type can significantly alter the means toward a happy life.

Notably, ENTPs do not want a stress-free life. In fact, what other types would consider a stress-free life sounds like a tedious nightmare to ENTPs.

A good argument and lively conflict bring them joy and energy. ENTPs do not want to be — and do not need to be — coddled by the world or the people around them. They want to be thrown into the fire. They may face failure after failure, but they would rather fail than never have tried.

Thus, for ENTPs to be happy, they need to live life to the fullest. They need to take risks and push boundaries. Although ENTPs can ignore rules, they will thrive in a flexible environment that respects their freethinking mind. They need the freedom to follow their impulses and whims.

Few ENTPs will be happy without a challenge. Depending on their preference, they may require a creative outlet, a problem to solve, an argument to win, or maybe, even all three. In any case, they do not want to swim in still waters. "Tranquility" is not a trait that comes to mind when thinking about what will bring an ENTP fulfillment. They always need a challenge to face.

Let us not forget the value of conversation. ENTPs love to talk. They like discourse, chatting, disagreements, debates—any conversation. ENTPs can only be happy if they have plenty of people to talk to. They can blissfully spend hours and days in pleasant conversation with a wide variety of individuals. ENTPs might consider discussion nearly as important as food. They must always seek it out, or their energy and happiness will suffer.

Finally, ENTPs need to be surrounded by the right people. In previous sections, it was said that ENTPs rely on others to turn their ideas into reality and manage the mundane details of their life. Whether it is a romantic partner, business partner, or just a reliable friend, no ENTP can reach their true potential without the "wind beneath their wings," as Bette Midler would say.

In general, ENTPs do not need to be told how to be happy. They are already living successful, happy lives, because it comes naturally to them. They do not let small, or even massive setbacks get them down, and will never sweat the minor details. They live life beyond the clouds and love every minute of it.

What are Some Common Careers for an ENTP?

ENTPs are in the fortunate position of being able to excel in a variety of careers. They can excel in the arts, sciences, business, education, law, and finance. There is hardly a field where an ENTP cannot find a good fit, as almost all disciplines need leaders and strategic, long-term thinkers. Additionally, the excellent people skills of ENTPs can help them succeed in any career that involves communication, which is almost all of them.

That, of course, is addressing what fields ENTPs might thrive in. Individual positions are a different story. If a job requires repetitive, lonely tasks with little challenge, like data entry, count an ENTP out. If the job is extremely detail-oriented and rigid with few opportunities for an ENTP to express their opinion, it will not be a good fit.

Many entry-level jobs are, for this reason, difficult for ENTPs, although they thrive at upper levels.

Politician

One of the most notable ENTPs living today was a politician, former President Barack Obama. ENTPs make great politicians at any level of government because they are charismatic, good at oral communication and public speaking, excellent in a debate, relatively immune to criticism, and strategic big-picture thinkers.

Furthermore, politicians, especially at higher levels, are visionaries and "idea people," just like ENTPs. They delegate to committees and cabinets where more detail-oriented subordinates can bring their visions to life.

Scientist

Some prominent scientists have been ENTPs. ENTP scientists will be theorists as opposed to interested in practical application. They have the capacity to see the world in new ways, and they possess the logic and determination to prove their theories and provide evidence for their discoveries.

ENTP scientists may not be interested in practical application—they will not be happy performing repetitive experiments to find out a small detail about something for product development, for example—but their inventiveness can come through and bring them great success.

Actor/Stand-Up Comedian

ENTPs love to be on stage. The more eyes on them, the better. They especially love the risk of a live audience. The taunts of a heckler will slide right off them as they easily deliver their lines or perform their routine. However, whether onstage or onscreen, they love to perform.

In fact, you could say that ENTPs even feed off criticism. They are invigorated by attention of all kinds—even negative attention. They are also not afraid to make shocking jokes and risk controversy, which means that ENTP comedians can get some of the biggest laughs in the business by taking their audiences completely off guard.

Comedy Writer

ENTPs are comfortable behind the camera or on stage, but they excel at writing the lines. More often than not, they choose positions where they can both write and perform, like stand up, as mentioned above.

Their wit is legendary, and they may be the wittiest of all the personality types. They see the humor in the mundane and can make light of difficult topics in clever ways. Their eloquence means that their delivery will also be impeccable.

However, you will not often find them writing solo projects. Working on a television show where they banter all day with a team of writers, or on an improv show where they take part in the action, however, is right up their alley.

Professor

Many prominent philosophers were ENTPs, including Socrates, Voltaire, and David Hume. However, "philosopher" is not exactly a realistic modern career path.

Today's professional thinkers are often professors teaching young minds, conducting research, or writing papers. ENTPs will not only enjoy getting to spend most of their time thinking, but they will also enjoy discourse with students and colleagues.

Teaching others may not be a priority for ENTPs, but if they must teach as part of their profession, they will do well since they are charismatic and great public speakers. Expect an ENTP professor to love lecturing and debate, but not to be great at organizing curriculum or walking students through details that they missed.

ENTP professors enjoy their students as debate partners and as an audience, rather than learners, most of the time.

Inventor

Three of the most notable ENTP inventors, Thomas Edison, Benjamin Franklin, and Leonardo da Vinci, have come up with countless inventions that have an impact in our daily life. ENTPs are ideal inventors because they never give up and can think about things in new ways. Furthermore, they have the logical thinking qualities needed to come up with ideas that can go a long way.

However, they often need a team or a partner to work out the details when creating a prototype, or they may become bored and move on to something else.

Lawyer

ENTPs love to argue and debate. They can easily take on any side of that debate and win just because they love the act and art of a strong argument. Thus, it is not hard to imagine why a career in law would be a good fit. They will thrive speaking in front of a courtroom and appreciate the challenge of convincing the judge and jury to think a certain way.

They are also immune to conflict and criticism, so being hated by the other side, or having to play hardball so that their client gets the best deal, excites them.

Inspirational Speaker

The skills of oration make ENTPs good politicians, but they do not have to be in an elected office to make a good speech. ENTPs are charismatic, persuasive, and thrive on a stage speaking to a large group. They also enjoy proposing new, dangerous ideas, and bringing others on board with their way of thinking.

They find it intoxicating when a group brings their way of thinking around to match the ENTPs, which makes them excellent motivational speakers. They will work very hard to entertain, cajole, and persuade their audience, using all of their charm, humor, and strength of personality to their fullest potential.

Talk Show Host

You cannot argue with facts. Although ENTPs make up only 3% of the population, they make up a surprisingly high percentage of talk show hosts. Conan O'Brian, Bill Maher, Jon Stewart, and Stephen Colbert are all ENTPs.

It is not that strange if you think about it. Talk show hosts are professional talkers! They are so good at conversation that they are hired to have conversations with influential people on camera. The hosts who manage hard-hitting topics are comfortable with a rousing argument with his guests. These qualities are all found in ENTPs.

No one job is perfect for any one personality type, but if there were, it would probably be having a career as a talk show host for ENTPs.

It is a job that provides everything most ENTPs crave. They experience the risk of offending an audience, losing ratings, or flubbing an interview. They have the adulation of the public. They are often confronted and debated with. They have the chance to articulate new, exciting, or even dangerous ideas. Their role does not require them to do anything particularly repetitive or detail oriented.

Entrepreneur

ENTPs are change makers in the arts and sciences, and they can also make waves in the business world. They are natural entrepreneurs, always coming up with grand new ideas and long-term strategic plans. They are not afraid to try new things. As such, they can create new businesses and ways of doing things. As long as they have some more practical people with them on the journey, they can easily create successful new business ventures.

ENTP entrepreneurs can have a runaway success if they are working on their own, but this requires coming up with a simple yet unique idea that sells well out of the box. For more elaborate business plans, ENTPs need a backup to handle details and organizational issues.

Sales

An ENTP loves to talk and to convince people to do things, or in this case, buy things. An ENTP can last eight hours or more a day talking to people and love it. They can influence and charm others. They are the type of people who believe they can sell anything to anyone, and they are usually right.

If you have ever had a marathon experience with a car salesman and wondered how they could still be talking even though you have voiced a dozen different objections and you found yourself second-guessing your opinions, you probably had a run-in with an ENTP!

Executive

An ENTP can make for a good leader of almost any venture. They see the big picture, think strategically, and love to innovate. Their charisma, confidence, and dominant personality make them a natural leader that others will follow.

Executives also have the advantage of having a staff that is specifically planned to take care of mundane tasks and details, which makes this a perfect position for the lofty idea loving, but detail-phobic ENTP.

Stock Broker/Venture Capitalist

ENTPs love risk. They love danger and excitement, and even a little chaos. They are not afraid to take big risks for the chance of big rewards and will not be bothered by losing money occasionally (even if they ought to be). They have the skills for thinking and analysis needed to make educated risks with a fair shot of paying off.

Journalist

ENTPs want to be where the action and adventure are, which makes them good candidates to become journalists. As a reporter, they will have the opportunity to go right into the center of the hurricane (literally or figuratively). In addition, they might get to ask many questions, including ones that can ruffle feathers.

They do not fear controversy; in fact, blowing the lid off a controversial story is exactly the sort of thing that an ENTP loves. The bustle of a newsroom and novelty of interviewing many different people about a wide variety of subjects suits them well. It is also a great opportunity for them to utilize their creative skills in a professional setting.

Consultant

Sometimes you just need a great idea. ENTPs can be good consultants on a variety of topics, including strategic planning, marketing, public relations, finance, urban planning, and more. They will not be that interested in sticking around to see the job be done anyway, so why not hire them just for the idea?

Although ENTPs have the opportunity to be successful in many roles, they can also easily find roles they will hate and do poorly in. Specifically, ENTPs will likely despise any role that requires routine, mundane tasks, attention to detail, and strict adherence to procedures. One could argue that those traits are important in almost all careers as well, and ENTPs have to find a way to deal with bureaucracy and structure. However, if they choose a job that leans more toward the creative and innovative, they will be much more successful.

Common Workplace Behaviors of an ENTP

The traits of an ENTP can be a double-edged sword in the workplace. If they are in a career that suits them, they can be astoundingly successful. However, if they are in a career that is a poor match, they will hate it and probably do a bad job. It is not uncommon for an ENTP to be viewed as the worst employee in the company in one job, but be seen as a rockstar in another position.

The keys to success in the workplace for the ENTP are creativity, challenge, and freedom. They need a job where they can come up with ideas and try new things. They need fresh new challenges on a regular basis to prevent boredom. More so, they need an environment without rigid rules and "red tape."

In the workplace, you will find the ENTP working on the "macro" level, meaning they are all about the big picture. They are full of ideas and big plans. You will not find them managing details like paperwork and files. If someone else does not take on those tasks, they may not be done at all.

You will also find ENTPs in charge or working in self-directed positions. Let us just say for ENTPs, it is "my way or the highway." They love getting to work with others, lead, and influence a team. However, they would rather work alone than be stifled by the seemingly arbitrary rules of another, even if they do not enjoy the solitude. They will usually find ways to socialize, anyway.

ENTPs are wildly innovative, and sometimes too much so. ENTPs are usually found "fixing" policies and trying new ways to do old things, even if it is not needed. Depending on your viewpoint, you might see them as subversive or non-conformist.

If you are an organized person, you will likely find the ENTP aggravating in the workplace. They might be late, disorganized, messy, distracted, and miss deadlines. This is particularly annoying because while they sincerely listen to criticism, it may seem like it has little effect on them (whether or not that is the case). They can even think in a scattered and unconventional way, which may seem chaotic to outsiders.

However, if given the right environment and role, an ENTP can be a fabulous and valuable addition to any workplace. Every business needs a big-picture. Thus, innovative thinkers like ENTPs are essential. As long as those traditional thinkers that are detail-oriented and handle the day-to-day responsibilities support them, the business will likely prosper.

ENTPs and Personal Relationships

As an extraverted type, ENTPs thrive on social connection. They love being with other people. In fact, they get their energy and power from interacting with others. As such, they actively seek out relationships and opportunities to engage in discussion and conversation.

Parenting Style & Values

ENTPs can be great parents that can foster strong young minds. They value knowledge and will give their child many opportunities to learn. They have open minds and will not be rigid about what passions their children should take on as long as their children are passionate about knowledge.

ENTP parents will not mind a child's endless questions. They never outgrew that child-like curiosity themselves. Thus, they greatly respect the child's need to understand the world.

Charismatic and vibrant, they are good at leading in

any situation, including leading a family. They will enjoy planning exciting and perhaps outlandish family vacations. ENTPs are the "fun parents." They are not concerned with rules and boundaries, so they might end up being too permissive. Their children's faces will always light up when they walk into the room, as they bring energy, adventure, and confidence that will enamor a child.

However, this is another reason why ENTPs need an opposing match for their co-parent. As single parents, they are likely to struggle with the required responsibility, rule setting, and household management.

ENTPs hate rules themselves and rely on persuasion and debate to get what they want from other adults, so they have a difficult time setting standards for their children. They have an even *harder* time enforcing them. After all, ENTPs do not mind conflict and rebellion, so they may dismiss rule-breaking without a second thought, allowing bad habits to develop.

Getting dinner on the table every night can turn into a parade of pizza and burgers with ENTPs (who often forget to feed themselves) that find themselves in the role of caregiver. Keeping up with extracurricular schedules is also a major challenge—children of ENTP parents quickly learn to keep track of when their sports practices and music lessons are.

They are happy to spend quality time with their children, but they may not necessarily be the ones spending quantity time. ENTPs will likely leave many of the more uninteresting details of parenting to their partner, too busy running off on adventures and following dreams to change diapers, do the laundry, and enforce a bedtime schedule.

Despite the challenges ENTPs face as parents, they are often beloved by their children and have no lack of love for their children in return. Even if Mom forgot to put the casserole in the oven, she always has a smile on her face and never makes a big deal out of an innocent mistake.

Friends

ENTPs can be fantastic friends. They love talking to people and have a genuine curiosity about others. They will be happy to get to know you and discuss your interests and thoughts. As such, ENTPs have no trouble making friends. People who want to be with them often surround them.

Although argumentative for fun, ENTPs are easy-going and tolerant. They are not "judging" types, so they like almost everyone. They are not easily offended and would certainly not let a minor disagreement derail a friendship.

When you talk to ENTPs, their curiosity and charm can make you feel like you are the most important person in the world, which feels great until you realize that you are not. ENTPs have scores of friends and will talk to anyone. Introverts may be shocked to learn that they are not as special to the ENTP as they are to them. It is easy for some types, especially INFPs, to be emotionally hurt by an ENTP. INFPs can be captivated by the ENTP quickly, but the ENTP will never be able to provide the emotional connection that the INFP needs.

ENTPs are also prone to "foot-in-mouth" disease. They are likely to say anything they want and love to make jokes. Thus, they can end up saying things that hurt feelings, even though they do not mean to do so.

With that said, other types could use ENTPs as a best friend, especially the ENTPs' introverted counterparts, such as the INTPs and INTJs. These types would love being close to the ENTP and taking part in their adventures. They would even be comfortable being "second-in-command" to the dominant ENTP. They can respect ENTPs' personality traits that others find annoying and thrive on the energy and enthusiasm that the ENTP injects into their life.

Romantic Partners

ENTPs can make wonderful life partners. They are energetic, charming, and never dull. You will enjoy a lifetime of engaging conversation and probably little adventures along the way.

ENTPs are best suited for mates who share their laid-back, low-stress approach to life. Types that are more neurotic may be initially drawn to the enigmatic, easy confidence of an ENTP, but their emotional needs might not be met. A feeling type personality will likely struggle with an ENTP as a partner because the ENTP will never quite respect or understand their deep feelings.

ENTPs are charming, eloquent, and spontaneous, so they can do well with romance, but they are not likely to be able to provide the genuine emotional connection that a "feeling" type will seek. Due to their charm and confidence, feeling types may be enamored by the ENTP only to end up getting hurt.

Although the "feeling" type may not be a good match, ENTPs are well suited for mates with opposing traits to provide the balance they need. They could use a partner with sensing and judging qualities to keep them grounded. An ISTJ could potentially be a good choice. They are very responsible types who excel at creating and enforcing order in chaos. However, they are not particularly emotional, so they can live the easy-going life the ENTP prefers. These two could make a great match with excellent balance, but could also aggravate each other. The key is to understand their differences and capitalizing on them by creating their unique roles in the relationship.

The Personality Page suggests INTJ or INFJ as good matches. Both types have the judging type to contrast the ENTP with a more actionable and focused side. However, they share the intuitive trait and may better appreciate the creativity and unique genius of the ENTP, since they can make decisions based on intuition.

ENTPs need that balance to keep them afloat, but there is plenty of room for conflict in a relationship with opposites—and their partner may not be as comfortable with conflict as they are. ENTPs are often the partners that neglect their share of household chores. At times, they may even ignore their partner if something else has captured their interest. Both the ENTP and their opposing partner must be willing to compromise for the pairing to work.

ENTPs have slightly lower marriage rates than other types. Meaning they can and will marry and have successful relationships, but they will also face challenges. ENTPs struggle with commitment. They are easily bored and love to move on to the next great thing. Unfortunately, this trait applies to both ideas and people.

They also might be prone to fight with their mate more than the average partner might. However, these "fights" will most likely be playful, easy banter. They do not have the emotional range to become truly furious; they simply like to argue. This can be good or bad, depending on their mate. INFPs, in particular, would find ENTPs annoying. INFPs hate and internalize conflict. Thus, the ENTP could traumatize an INFP with their playful banter.

If you manage to get an ENTP to stay in one place, the ENTP will fill your life with energy and adventure. They are enthusiastic life partners who will view relationships as less of an emotional support, but as another way to explore life. They are curious about love and sex, and although they will not be interested in their partner's feelings, they are very interested in their partner's interests and thoughts.

8 Actionable Steps for Overcoming Your Weaknesses as an ENTP

Weaknesses are part of being human. We all have them. Many of the world's most successful people are dripping in flaws. However, the key to success is not being perfect but finding ways to keep your flaws from standing in the way to your success.

1. Find the Right Mate

ENTPs need people in their life, much more than most types. Without someone to keep them grounded, they will spend their lives floating in the clouds and not getting things done. Bills will not be paid, dishes will go unwashed, and all sorts of other details will be ignored. A balanced life requires the loving support of another person to round up the ENTPs and provide balance.

ENTPs can occasionally appear aloof, lack respect for feelings, and say hurtful things. They also struggle with commitment. This puts ENTPs in the dangerous situation of needing a partner, yet also highly prone to losing that partner. Thus, it is critical that ENTPs respect and honor their partner with full awareness of how much they need them. If ENTPs choose to do so, they have all the tools to make that person feel loved and valued. They can charm them with words, show a genuine interest, and essentially be easy to fall in love with. ENTPs should use these skills to keep their mate as happy as possible.

2. Mind the Details

They say "the devil is in the details," and that may be especially true for ENTPs. Although for them, you might say that their downfall is in the details. Big-picture, macro-level thinking is essential for innovation and creation, but the tiniest detail can derail everything.

Ignoring details can be the pitfall of ENTPs. They have no respect for the importance of details and will miss the ones that matter. ENTPs will never be detail-oriented, but they can learn to be more aware of details. The key is for them to understand which details are important and which ones they can let go. If ENTPs have a good sense of what to look for, they can grasp the important details around them without battling against the natural instincts of their personality type.

3. Pick Your Battles

ENTPs can appear negative and argumentative simply because they love to argue. ENTPs need to be more careful about whom they argue with and what topics they choose. Not everyone will enjoy the playful banter like they do. If they start the wrong argument, they can lose friends, or harm their career or marriage.

On a similar note, ENTPs can be too resistant to rules and restrictions. They do not see them as important and will rebel against them. A failure to follow the rules can obviously cause problems in their career, and perhaps even lead them to break laws. ENTPs need to ask themselves if rules are worth breaking. If the rule is unimportant, why not follow it? ENTPs might consider the rule to be an obstacle to their goal, but breaking the rule might create bigger obstacles for them than the rule itself.

4. Respect the Contribution of Others

Walt Disney knew that his dreams would never have come alive without the contributions of others, and all ENTPs should keep this in mind. ENTPs have big, sweeping dreams that require the effort of all 16 types to get in motion.

If ENTPs work alone, they are unlikely to get much done. They are thinkers and dreamers, not doers. They cannot function without the support of other types. ENTPs would be wise to use their natural charisma and sparkling personality to charm everyone around them and make them feel valued. ENTPs need helpers, and they should make sure those people feel and know exactly how much they are needed.

5. Use Your Talents Wisely

ENTPs can do amazing things, so why waste your time and energy? ENTPs can be prone to inefficiency — simply spinning their wheels and getting nowhere. They should not fall into that rut. ENTPs are logical beings, and even though they might have natural inclinations to chase rainbows, they should remind themselves that there is not a pot of gold at the end. ENTPs must pursue a dream that matters.

ENTPs enjoy innovation for the sake of innovation and may waste time re-inventing the wheel. They also struggle with sticking with a project. One so-so idea that becomes a reality is better than a million brilliant ideas that are left half done. If they are inclined to move away from a project before it is done, they should remind themselves that those half-baked ideas are not worth anything. ENTPs are smart and logical, and they should know how to take the next steps, so they should generate the willpower to stick with one thing until it is finished.

6. Consider the Feelings of Others

Feelings can be such an inconvenient obstacle. You do not understand why feelings are so important to others, and you do not understand why they have so many of the darn things in the first place. You do not get your feelings hurt easily, but you are unique in that way. However, almost everyone around you is more prone to hurt, embarrassment, and offense than you are.

As with rules, you may find that feelings are not important enough to focus on, but as also with rules, you are going to create greater obstacles for yourself if you ignore feelings. Like details and regulations, feelings are a necessary burden for you. You cannot afford to ignore them. Your intuitive side understands that people make decisions based on feelings and "gut," and those feelings can alter their choices in ways that could significantly impact your latest dream or idea. Your general belief that feelings are not important does not mean that they are not. Again, use your natural charm and conversational skills to ask about feelings so that the people around you understand that they have been heard.

7. Make Compromises

Here is the bottom line -- ENTPs cannot function in the world if they do not make compromises. Despite figuratively having their heads in the clouds, ENTPs' bodies are stuck firmly in reality, whether they like it or not. They live in a world where minor details like paying bills and meeting deadlines can have a critical impact on their lives. They live in a world with rules and boundaries that will not disappear just because ENTPs do not like them.

ENTPs can use their big-picture thinking to their advantage in this case. Focus on the end-result or vision. The means that getting there is not what is important. Sometimes the means to the end includes rules and boring details. Do not let your aversion to such things sabotage your vision.

8. Follow Rules

No, not all the time. We need ENTPs to challenge standards and convention so that our society can progress. However, there is no point in breaking the rules just for the sake of breaking the rules. Be careful to resist rules and structure only if there is a compelling reason to do so. Otherwise, you will only hurt yourself and others. You could even lose your job or go to jail. Do not ruin yourself to break a rule unless it is worth it.

If ENTPs completely shun rules and rigid environments, they might also miss some great adventures and leadership opportunities, like the military. Truity said,

"And it may come as a bit of a surprise, but the military can often be a good fit for the ENTP. Though they will be frustrated by what they see as excessive rules, guidelines, and exercise of authority, ENTPs will be very drawn to the variety, adaptability, strategizing, and responsibility that a career in the armed forces involves."

In many ways, this section is the most important. ENTPs can be brilliant successes that change history, but they are also prone to make disastrous mistakes. The key to success with all types, and with ENTPs especially, is to learn to live with your flaws and do not let them get in your way.

The 12 Most Influential ENTPs We Can Learn From

Skimming the list below, you can see that ENTPs have left a significant mark on our culture in art, science, film, and politics. ENTPs are the world's change-makers. In fact, it is hard to limit the list of influential leaders to only 12 as ENTPs have made a tremendous impact on society since ancient times. It is especially surprising that so many influential people are ENTPs because they only make up for 3% of the population. That supports the contention that ENTPs shine a little brighter and are more likely to rise to the top.

This already rare personality type is even rarer among women. Only 2% of women are ENTPs. As such, it is impressive that many famous women are among the group, specifically actresses, singers, and comedians. It is proof that ENTPs of both genders are likely to rise above the fray. As only one woman was represented on the list, but other famous women who are ENTPs include Celine Dion, Salma Hayek, Sarah McLaughlin, Amy Poehler, Gillian Anderson, Elizabeth Olsen, Rose McGowan, Claire Danes, and Megan Mullally. Since it is impossible to list all famous ENTPs, the list is restricted to the following 12 people who are considered the most influential ENTPs that have brought change to the world.

1. Barack Obama

The 44th President of the United States and the first African-American to hold the office is a prime example of an immensely successful ENTP. Charismatic, a legendary orator, and seemingly unflappable, he exhibits many of the classic ENTP characteristics. He is also a dreamer. The cornerstones of his campaign were "hope" and "change." Consider the title of his second book, *The Audacity of Hope: Reclaiming the American Dream.* Obama believes in the impossible and is not afraid to chase after it.

2. Thomas Edison

The famous inventor of the light bulb held over 1,000 patents and is another textbook perfect example of an ENTP. Edison specifically demonstrates the ENTPs' ability to think in new ways and never give up. While he is known for his significant successes, he was also known for his ability to fail. He attempted wild inventions such as a device that can speak to the dead wherein he failed, of course. Edison is famous for having said, "I have not failed 10,000 times. I have not failed once. I have succeeded in proving that those 10,000 ways will not work. When I have eliminated the ways that will not work, I will find the way that will work."

3. Walt Disney

Another poster child for ENTPs, Walt Disney, was the ultimate dreamer and believer in the impossible. Although his massive success in film and theme parks make him a legend, he is no stranger to failure. He began his first production studio in 1923, and it failed miserably, leaving him bankrupt. However, he did not give up, and only a few years later, he created Mickey Mouse. Walt Disney is well-known for believing in dreams and having the courage and tenacity to make them a reality.

4. Benjamin Franklin

The famous founding father and familiar face from the twenty-dollar bill was an innovative thinker and a jack-of-all-trades. He pioneered all sorts of things: libraries, fire departments, paper money, bifocals, swim fins, lightning rods, and musical instruments. He also attempted some unnecessary innovations such as when he proposed to remove letters C, J, Q, W, X and Y from the alphabet. Like all ENTPs, he was not afraid to fail, famously saying, "Do not fear mistakes. You will know failure. Continue to reach out."

5. Leonardo da Vinci

The artist made a significant contribution to the Italian

Renaissance. In fact, he practically *was* the Italian Renaissance. Although known for his classic works such as the Mona Lisa and The Last Supper, he was also an inventor. He wrote 13,000 pages worth of innovative ideas, including a "flying machine" more than 400 years before the actual invention of the airplane. In ENTP style, most of his inventions were only theories that he never applied. If he had followed through with the "flying machine" and other medical theories, we can only wonder what he might have accomplished. He even had a practical sidekick to keep his house in order, his assistant and possible lover, Francesco Melzi.

6. Jon Stewart

The pioneer of entertainment news, Jon Stewart of The Daily Show has many significant attributes of an ENTP. He is quick-witted, charismatic, comfortable in an argument, and not afraid to say things that might offend.

However, Jon Stewart is far more than a wordsmith with a sense of humor. Jeremy Cayman once described him as being able to take "vast" ideas and concepts and distil them. He can transform the big picture—no matter how complex—into something "manageable" and clear for others. This is the key to his talent for simultaneously revealing the humor and horror in the world.

7. Bill Maher

Bill Maher embodies the ENTP's argumentative nature and disregard for political correctness. In fact, he became famous for his show entitled *Politically Incorrect with Bill Maher*. Like most ENTPs, he sees dissent and criticism as constructive paths to improvement. When accused of being unpatriotic, he responded that his critique of the nation was *how* he exercised his patriotism, asking how anyone could expect something to improve without first identifying its flaws. Although he may offend some people, he is correct in his belief that we need those individuals who are willing to question things without caring, whether it may hurt people or not. Like many ENTPs, he can sometimes cross the line. In 2002, he made controversial comments about the 9/11 terrorist attacks that ultimately got his show canceled.

8. Richard Feynman

This scientist was best known for his work in quantum mechanics and particle physics and was one of the creators of the atomic bomb as part of the Manhattan Project. His ENTP personality is highlighted in many ways, but his zest for creativity and innovation, discovery, and exploration, is particularly prominent. He once described the search for new scientific laws as something that inspired excitement in him because of the idea that he might be thinking of a possibility that no one had ever contemplated in the past.

9. Chairman Mao

Communist Dictator Mao Tse-Tung provides a cautionary example of how ENTPs can make critical errors. Although his means were often violent, Mao was an idealist and a dreamer like his ENTP counterparts. As part of the "Great Leap Forward," he set nearly astounding and unbelievable goals for agriculture and industry.

However, his big dreams turned out to be both impossible and deadly. During the "Great Leap Forward," forty million Chinese citizens died of hunger. He rose through the ranks with his charisma and big thinking, but it was eventually evident that he has no ability to manage a country — fitting the ENTP trait of being great leaders, but terrible managers.

10.   Julia Child

Julia child was a fabulous chef, and she was also a sparkling personality, fitting well with many other television host ENTPs. Although seemingly dull for a

119

television star, she inspired others with her confidence, humor, and honesty. Julie Powell, the author of the cooking blog that inspired the movie *Julie and Julia*, said, "Her voice and her attitude and her playfulness... it is just magical. You cannot fake that. You cannot take classes to learn how to be wonderful." In classic ENTP style, Julia also did not put much stock in feelings, fear, or inhibitions.

11. Socrates

The ultimate philosopher, Socrates, proposed a moral system based on human reason over theology, which was a dangerously controversial idea at the time. He was known for his dialogues and ability to challenge others. The "Socratic method," named after him, is a style of learning based on questioning and debate. In many ways, he introduced the entire concept of critical thinking.

He is lesser known for some of his other ENTP qualities, such as being an aggravating husband. His wife was said to have complained that he provided no practical assistance as a philosopher and did not assist with parenting and household duties. Instead, he was only interested in thought and discourse.

He was so courageous and stubborn that his unconventional thinking led to his death. He was executed for his "crimes" and was witty until the end, suggesting that instead of killing him, the jury should commend him for his enlightening the minds of the townsfolk and reimburse him for his services.

12. Theodore Roosevelt

The war hero and President was also a visionary. He turned his love of nature into the beginning of the environmentalist movement. He spearheaded the ambitious national park system, which was a very different kind of thinking in a time that focused on industry and progress. He was also well-known for being energetic, charismatic, and adventurous.

Conclusion

ENTPs are magical people, or as close to magic as we have in our reality. Even Julie Powell referred to her ENTP idol, Julia Child, as "magical." Consider the magicians in our world that have brought dreams to reality like Walt Disney. Then there are the enchanting ENTPs like Leonardo da Vinci, whose work has sparked mystery and wonder for centuries.

ENTPs can do amazing things that change our world. If your personality falls into this category, respect the contribution that you can offer and find your best fit. If you love an ENTP, understand their flaws and honor their strengths.

ENTPs may never be organized, focused, and detail-oriented, but that is okay. They can fill the world with beautiful, amazing, and impossible things. The ENTP may never understand feelings, but they can inspire an entire nation with their powerful charisma and oratorical prowess. ENTPs may not be able to pay bills on time, but they can break the boundaries of our world — realizing the impossible.

Their courageousness and willingness to fail can make them some of our most spectacular failures, and our greatest successes. ENTPs have made a significant mark on history, and the young ENTPs are now on deck. Who knows what they will have in store for us if we foster their strengths and embrace their unique role in society?

Final Word/About the Author

I was born and raised in Norwalk, Connecticut. Growing up, I could often be found spending afternoons reading in the local public library about management techniques and leadership styles, along with overall outlooks towards life. It was from spending those afternoons reading about how others have led productive lives that I was inspired to start studying patterns of human behavior and self-improvement. Usually I write works around sports to learn more about influential athletes in the hopes that from my writing, you the reader can walk away inspired to put in an equal if not greater amount of hard work and perseverance to pursue your goals. However, I began writing about psychology topics such as the Myers Brigg Type Indicator so that I could help others better understand why they act and think the way they do and how to build on their strengths while also identifying their weaknesses. If you enjoyed *ENTP: Understanding & Relating with the Inventor,* please leave a review! Also, you can read more of my general works on *Gratitude, How to Fundraise, How to Get Out of the Friend Zone, Histrionic Personality Disorder, Narcissistic Personality Disorder, Avoidant Personality Disorder, Sundown Syndrome, ISTJs, ISFJs, ISFPs, INTJs, INFPs, INFJs, ESFPs, ESFJs, ESTJs, ENFPs, ENFJs, ENTJs, How to be Witty, How to be Likeable, How to be Creative, Bargain Shopping, Productivity Hacks, Morning Meditation, Becoming a Father,* and *33 Life Lessons: Success Principles, Career Advice & Habits of Successful People* in the Kindle Store.

Like what you read? Please leave a review!

I write because I love sharing personal development information on topics like why people behave the way they do with fantastic readers like you. My readers inspire me to write more so please do not hesitate to let me know what you thought by leaving a review! If you love books on life, basketball, or productivity, check out my website at claytongeoffreys.com to join my exclusive list where I let you know about my latest books. Aside from being the first to hear about my latest releases, you can also download a free copy of *33 Life Lessons: Success Principles, Career Advice & Habits of Successful People*. See you there!

Clayton

Bibliography

Barack Obama. (2015). Retrieved from A&E Television Networks.

Benjamin Franklin. (2015). Retrieved from A&E Television Networks.

Bill Maher. (2015). Retrieved from A&E Television Networks.

Caunt, B. S., Franklin, J., Brodaty, N. E., & Brodaty, H. (2012). Exploring the causes of subjective well-being: A content analysis of people's recipes for long-term happiness. *Journal of Happiness Studies* , 475-99.

Edison, T. (2015). Retrieved from A&E Television Networks.

Elias, M. (2002, December 8). *USA TODAY: Latest World and US News*. Retrieved from USA Today.

ENTP relationships. (n.d.). Retrieved from The personality page.

Famous ENTPs. (n.d.). Retrieved from CelebrityTypes.com.

Furr, N. (2011, June 9). *How Failure Taught Edison to Repeatedly Innovate*. Retrieved from Forbes.

Gaille, B. (2013, August 5). *List of 44 famous people with the ENTP personality type*. Retrieved from BrandonGaille.com.

Hoeller, C. (2013, December 5). *ENTPs Make Poor Managers but Exceptional Leaders*. Retrieved from Backwards Time Machine.

Krantz, D., & McCeney, M. K. (2002). Effects of psychological and social factors on organic disease: A critical assessment of research on coronary heart disease. *Annual Review of Psychology* , 341-69.

Leonardo da Vinci. (2015). Retrieved from A&E Television Networks.

Mao Tse-Tung. (2015). Retrieved from A&E Television Networks.

Myers, I. B., & Myers, P. B. (1980). *Gifts differing: Understanding personality type.* Mountain View, CA: CPP.

Owens, M. (2012). *ENTP: Portrait of an Inventor.*

Parker-Pope, T. (2010, April 17). *Is Marriage Good for Your Health?* Retrieved from The New York Times.

Perez, A. (2013, October 30). *16 Walt Disney Quotes To Help Guide You Through Life*. Retrieved from Buzzfeed.

Richard Feynman. (2015). Retrieved from A&E Television Networks.

Socrates. (2015). Retrieved from A&E Television Networks.

Thomas A. Edison Quotes. (n.d.). Retrieved from Author of diary and sundry observations of Thomas Edison.

(2014). Introduction to the ENTP. In Truity, *The True ENTP.* Truity Psychometrics LLC.

Walt Disney. (2015). Retrieved from A&E Television Networks.

Walt Disney Quotes. (n.d.). Retrieved from BrainyQuote.

Made in the USA
San Bernardino, CA
21 October 2017